ENGINEERING ANSWERS

How Light Switches Brighten a Room

BY MEGAN GENDELL

An Imprint of Abdo Publishing
abdobooks.com

abdobooks.com

Published by Abdo Publishing, a division of ABDO, PO Box 398166, Minneapolis, Minnesota 55439.

Printed in the United States of America, North Mankato, Minnesota.
102024
012025

Cover Photo: Vladimir Sukhachev/Shutterstock Images
Interior Photos: Shutterstock Images, 4–5, 10–11, 13, 14, 17 (circuits), 17 (off switch), 17 (on switch), 22, 25, 26, 29; iStockphoto, 6, 12; Universal History Archive/Universal Images Group/Getty Images, 8; Eakrin Rasadonyindee/Shutterstock Images, 18; Somchai Som/Shutterstock Images, 20–21, 28

Editor: Marley Richmond
Series Designer: Laura Kuchar

Library of Congress Control Number: 2024938356

Publisher's Cataloging-in-Publication Data

Names: Gendell, Megan, author.
Title: How light switches brighten a room / by Megan Gendell
Description: Minneapolis, Minnesota: ABDO Publishing, 2025 | Series: Engineering answers | Includes online resources and index.
Identifiers: ISBN 9781098295875 (lib. bdg.) | ISBN 9798384916871 (ebook)
Subjects: LCSH: Engineering--Juvenile literature. | Electric lighting--Juvenile literature. | Illumination--Juvenile literature. | Electrical engineering--Juvenile literature. | Questions and answers--Juvenile literature. | Engineering design--Juvenile literature.
Classification: DDC 620.1--dc23

CONTENTS

Some rooms have more than one light switch. Each switch may control a different light.

CHAPTER 1

Flip a Switch

It is the middle of the night. Nora is wide awake. She thinks reading for a little while will help her fall asleep. But the house is dark.

Nora walks to the door and moves her hand across the wall. Her fingers hit the light switch.

Lamps have controls that turn them on and off. These controls open and close an electrical circuit. Electricity reaches the lamp through a wire connected to an outlet in the wall.

She can feel that it is pointing down toward the floor. She flips it up.

Moving the switch from *off* to *on* closes an electrical **circuit**. This makes electricity flow through wires behind the wall and ceiling. They connect to a light bulb. Electricity moves through the wires and reaches the light. The light bulb begins to glow, and the room brightens.

Now Nora can see. She picks up her book. After Nora reads a few pages, her eyelids feel heavy. She's ready to go to bed. She walks over to the wall and flips the light switch down.

Moving the switch from *on* to *off* opens the electrical circuit. This stops electricity from flowing through the wires. Electricity cannot reach the bulb. The ceiling light turns off.

The room is dark again. Nora climbs into bed and pulls up the covers. She falls back to sleep.

Toggle Light Switch

A light switch that flips on and off is called a toggle light switch. This type of switch was invented in 1917. Before that, most light switches had two buttons. A person pushed the top button to turn a light on. Below that was another button to turn the light off.

Early light switches looked much different than toggle switches today. A handle was flipped to the right or left to control this type of switch.

Kinds of Switches

Light switches allow people to turn lights on and off. Light switches are often found in homes, schools, offices, and other indoor spaces.

Engineer John Henry Holmes invented the first light switch in 1884.

Switches control more than just lights. They can turn many electric items on or off, such as flashlights, ceiling fans, or toys. These switches may be connected to batteries. But they work the same way. When the switch is on, electricity flows and the item works. When the switch is off, electricity cannot flow.

Further Evidence

Look at the website below. What new evidence does it give to support Chapter One?

Electric Circuit

abdocorelibrary.com/light-switches-brighten

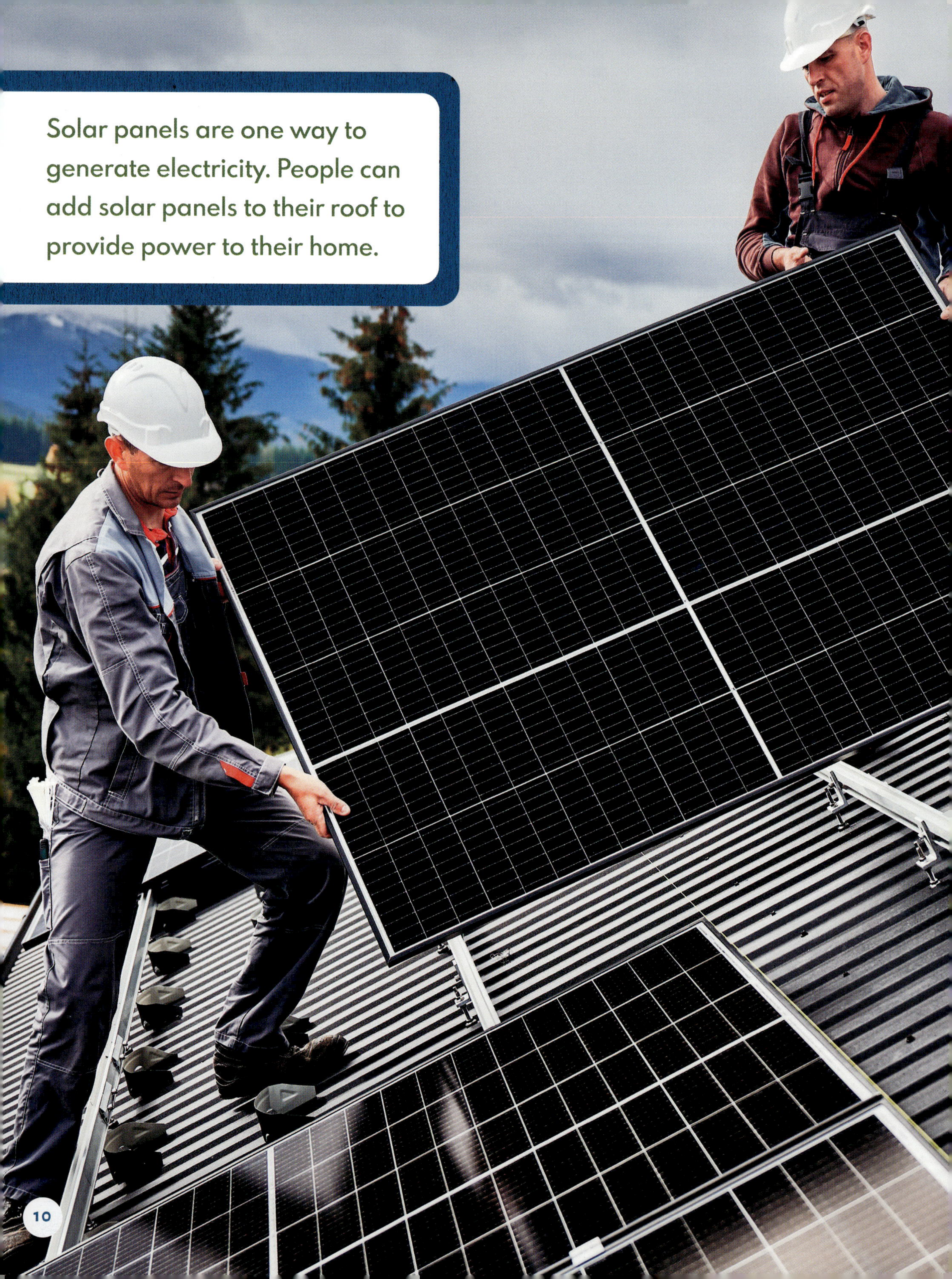

Solar panels are one way to generate electricity. People can add solar panels to their roof to provide power to their home.

CHAPTER 2

Electricity and Circuits

Electricity is a type of energy. People **generate** electricity to power many things. Electricity comes from **particles** that are so small that humans can't see them. These particles are called **atoms**.

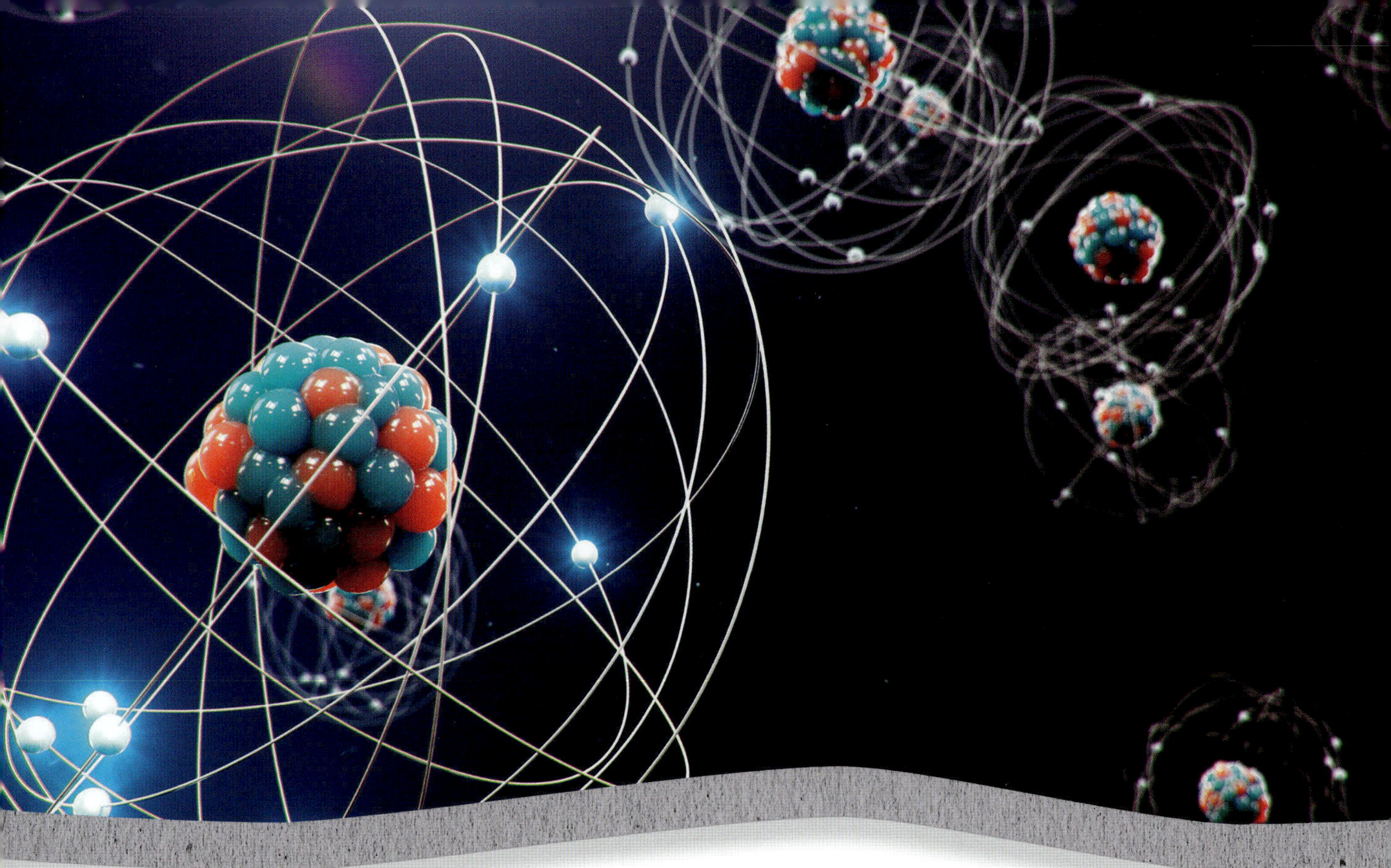

Scientific drawings show how electrons move around the center of an atom. Electrons can jump from one atom to another nearby atom.

Everything in the universe is made of atoms. Atoms have a center. Moving around that center are even smaller particles called electrons. Sometimes electrons jump from one atom to another. The movement of electrons between atoms is called electricity.

Many power plants use natural gas. These plants burn fuel to generate electricity.

Electrons are everywhere, all the time. But they don't always move from one atom to another. For electricity to flow to a light, two things are needed. The first is a power source. The second is a closed circuit.

Power Sources

Power sources push electricity to where it is needed. Power plants are one power source. These are big factories that create voltage.

Power lines bring energy from power plants to other buildings.

Voltage is the pressure that pushes electrons and makes them flow. Power plants push electricity through wires. These wires may carry electricity for miles. They connect to many buildings.

A battery is another a power source. It also pushes electrons through wires connected to it.

Light Speed

Electricity travels a little slower than the speed of light, which is about 980 million feet per second (300 million m/s). When a person flips a light switch, electricity travels to the light bulb very quickly. The light comes on so fast that it looks like the light turns on instantly.

When a person switches on a flashlight, the flashlight battery pushes electricity through wires to the light bulb. Batteries store limited amounts of electricity. When they run out of power, batteries must be charged or replaced.

Circuits

Electricity is pushed from a power source along a pathway. This path is called a circuit. A circuit allows electricity to travel from the power source to a light or other item that uses power.

For electricity to power a light bulb, the circuit must have no gaps or openings. A complete circuit is said to be closed. When part of this pathway is broken or missing, the circuit is said to be open. Electricity cannot flow if a

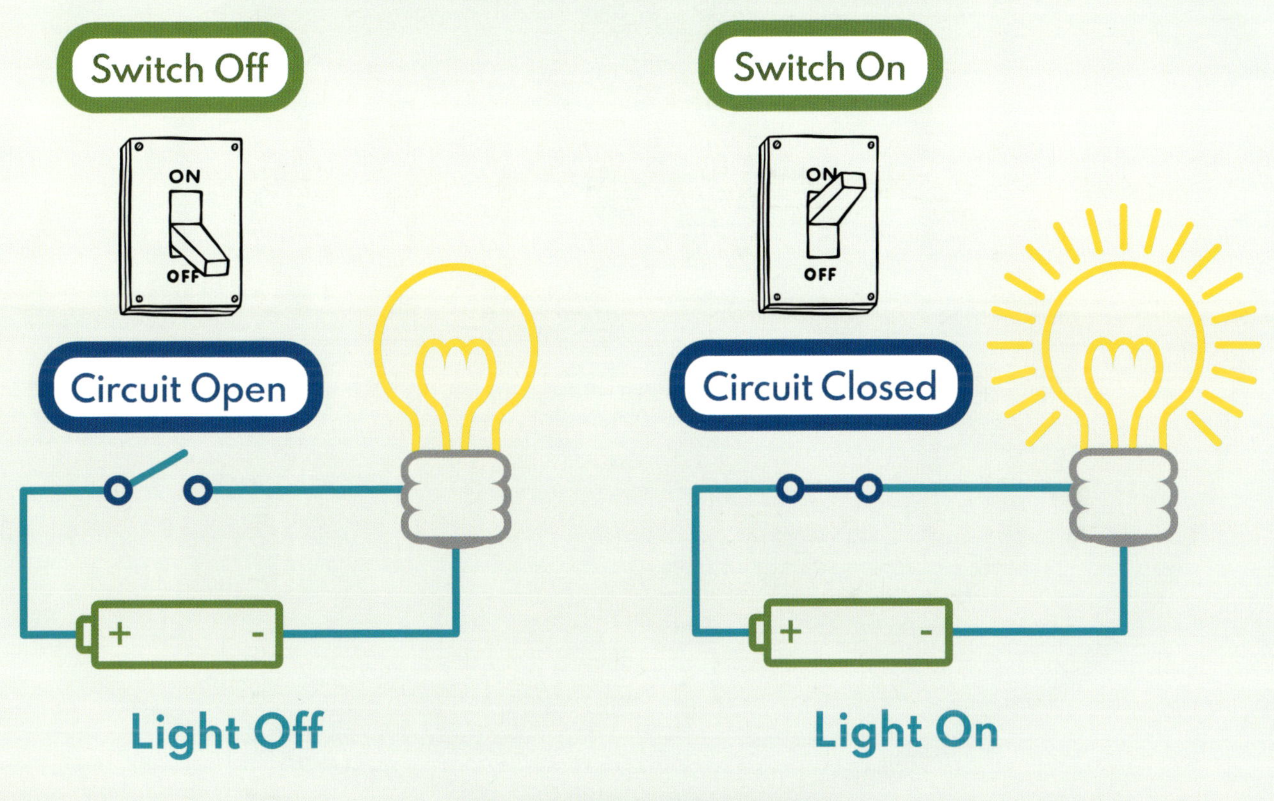

Light switches open and close circuits to control light bulbs.

circuit is open. The place where the pathway is broken creates a dead end.

A light switch opens and closes a circuit. The circuit allows electricity to reach a light bulb.

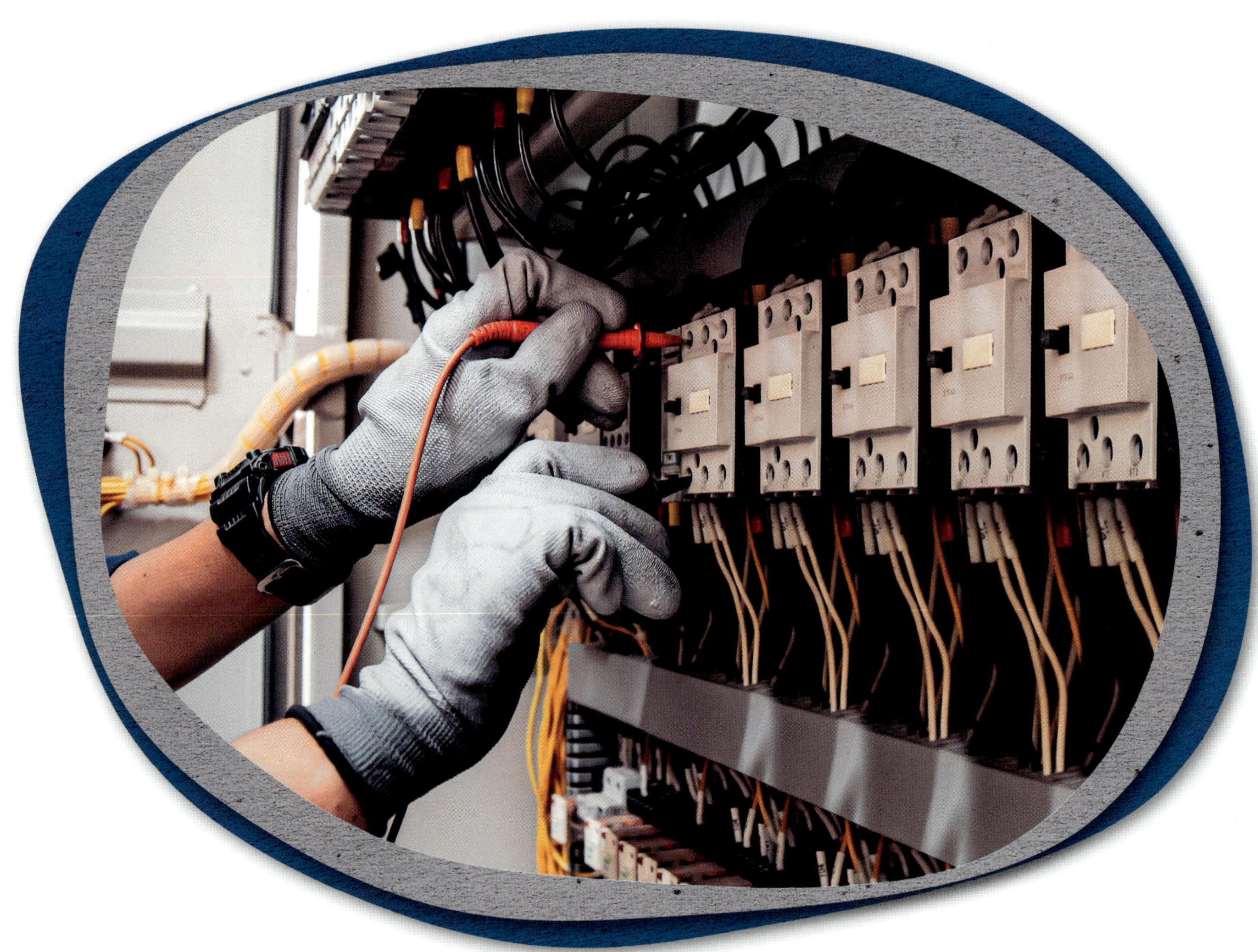

Light switches are connected to wires that create an electrical circuit. Electricians fix these wires if anything goes wrong.

When someone flips the switch on, it closes the circuit. Electricity flows to the light bulb, and the bulb lights up. When the circuit is opened, electricity stops flowing. The light turns off.

Primary Source

Paul Hines is an electrical engineer and a professor at the University of Vermont. He says:

> Electricity is the flow of electrons. Electrons are one of the basic building blocks of the universe. . . . Whenever those electrons start moving, that's electricity.

Source: Melody Bodette and Jane Lindholm. "What Is Electricity?" *But Why*, 15 July 2019, vermontpublic.org. Accessed 3 Mar. 2024.

What's the Big Idea?

Read this quote carefully. What is its main idea? Explain how the main idea is supported by details.

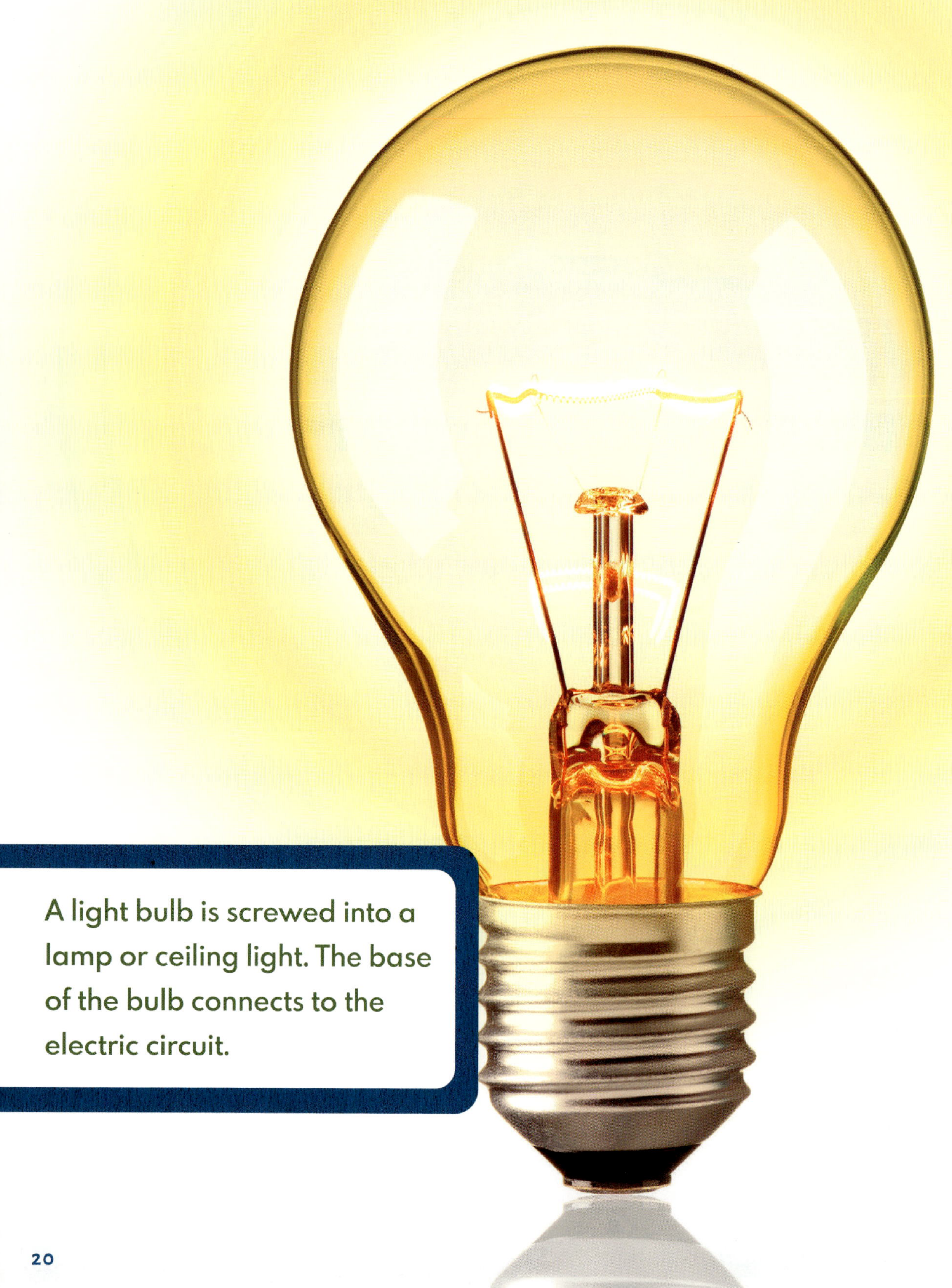

A light bulb is screwed into a lamp or ceiling light. The base of the bulb connects to the electric circuit.

CHAPTER 3

Light Bulbs

When a light switch is flipped on, electricity flows to the light bulb. Electricity enters most bulbs through the base. Next, electricity moves through the part of the bulb that lights up. Then it flows back out of the bulb through the side of the metal base.

Many common light bulbs use about 6.5 feet (2 m) of filament. The thin metal is wound into a coil. The coil is less than 1 inch (2.5 cm) long.

Incandescent Bulbs

Different types of light bulbs work in different ways. The incandescent bulb was invented in the late 1800s. These bulbs have a filament. This is a thin thread of metal. Electricity makes this metal get very hot. When the filament gets hot enough, it glows. The bulb lights up.

If this filament were exposed to air, it would burn. Then it would break and stop glowing. Air contains oxygen, which can make things burn quickly. This is why the filament is inside a glass bulb. The bulb is usually filled with gas that has no oxygen. Without oxygen, the filament burns much slower.

After glowing for hundreds of hours, a filament will melt. The filament gets thinner and weaker. Finally, it breaks. The light bulb stops working and needs to be replaced.

LED Bulbs

Light-emitting diodes, or LEDs, are a newer type of bulb. LEDs were invented in 1962. These bulbs are gaining popularity.

They last longer and use less energy than incandescent bulbs.

In LED bulbs, electricity passes through a **semiconductor**. This material glows but does not get very hot. Semiconductors use less energy than filaments to create the same amount of light. Using less electricity is better for the environment.

Fuels

Many power plants burn coal or natural gas to create voltage. Earth has a limited amount of these fuels. If humans use too much, supplies could run out. Burning these fuels also releases gases that harm the environment. Using less electricity helps keep Earth healthy.

LEDs can produce many different colors of light.

Many people choose LED bulbs instead of incandescent bulbs because they are better for the environment.

The materials inside LED bulbs can glow for a long time. Semiconductors don't burn up the way filaments do. LEDs can last for up to 50,000 hours. This is much longer than incandescent bulbs. So LED bulbs don't need to be replaced as often. They create less waste.

When a person flips a light switch on, a lot happens in the blink of an eye. The switch closes a circuit. Electricity flows to a light bulb. A filament or semiconductor begins to glow. This process lights up rooms all around the world.

Explore Online

Visit the website below. Does it give any new information about how light bulbs work that wasn't in Chapter Three?

What Makes a Light Bulb Light Up?

abdocorelibrary.com/light-switches-brighten

Engineering Facts

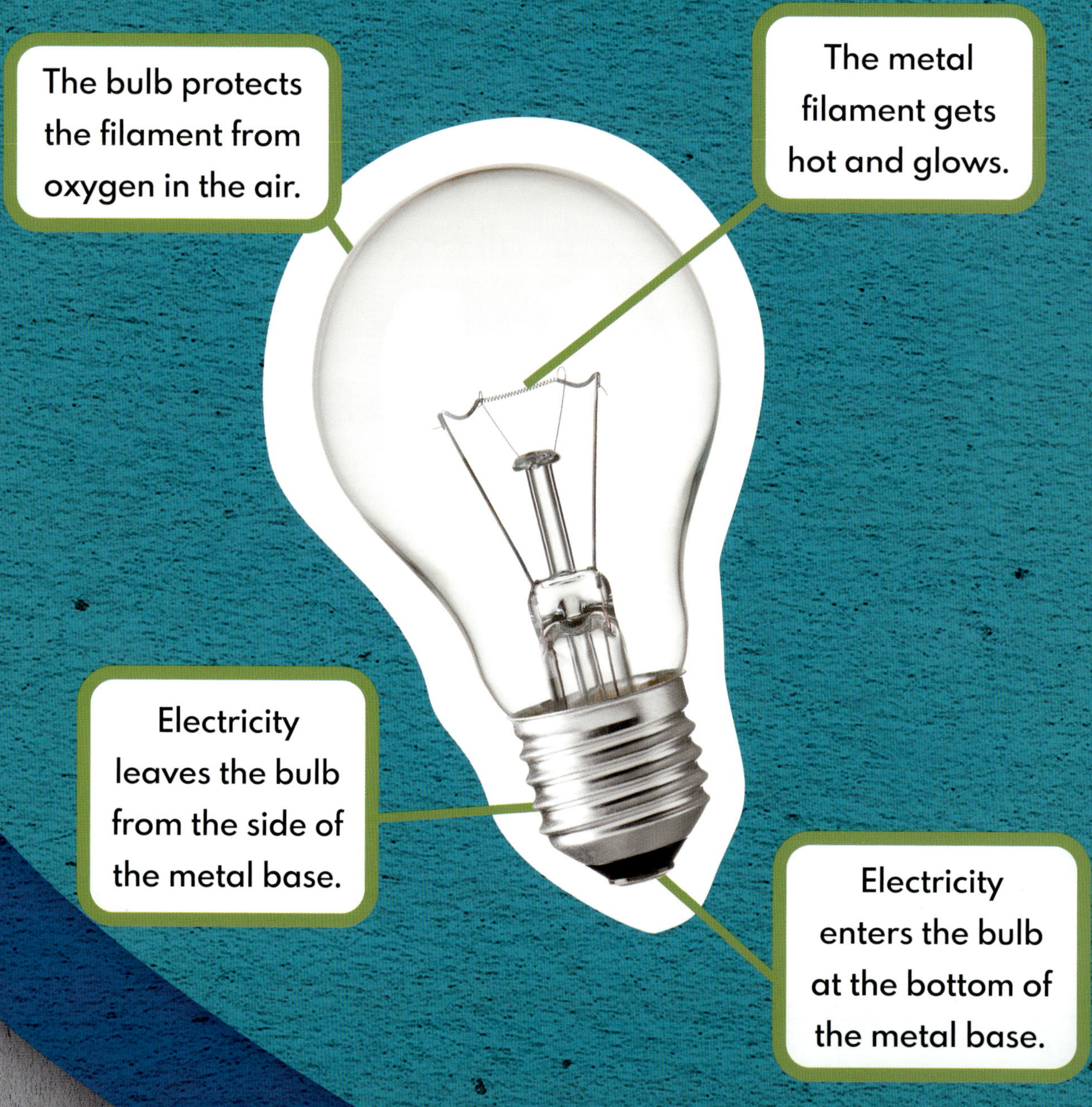

The bulb protects the filament from oxygen in the air.

The metal filament gets hot and glows.

Electricity leaves the bulb from the side of the metal base.

Electricity enters the bulb at the bottom of the metal base.

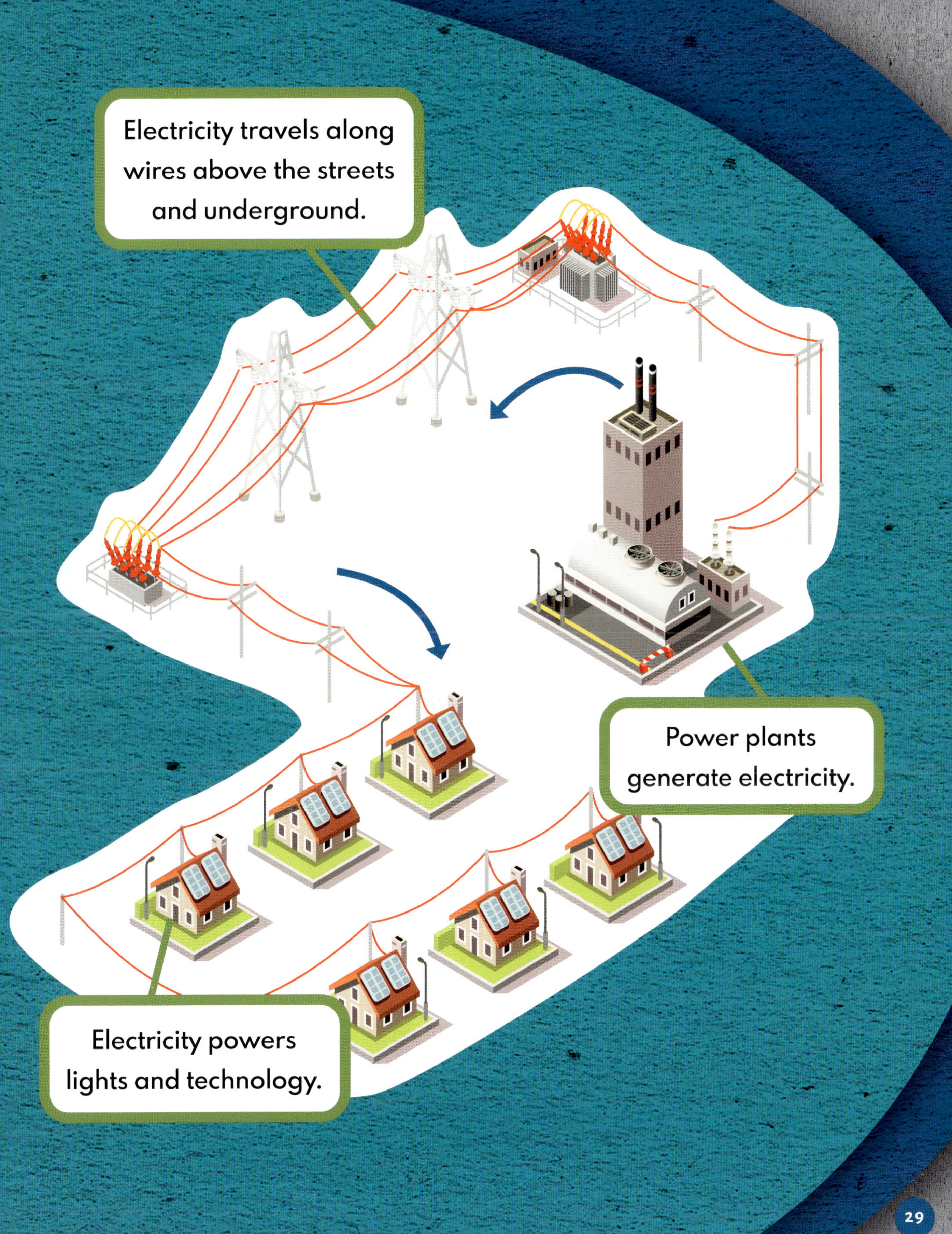
Electricity travels along wires above the streets and underground.
Power plants generate electricity.
Electricity powers lights and technology.

Glossary

atom
a tiny particle that makes up everything in the universe

circuit
a path along which electricity can travel

engineer
a person who is trained to design and build machines and structures

generate
to produce

particles
very small parts of something

semiconductor
a material through which electricity can flow under specific conditions

Online Resources

To learn more about light switches, visit our free resource websites below.

Visit **abdocorelibrary.com** or scan this QR code for free Common Core resources for teachers and students, including vetted activities, multimedia, and booklinks, for deeper subject comprehension.

Visit **abdobooklinks.com** or scan this QR code for free additional online weblinks for further learning. These links are routinely monitored and updated to provide the most current information available.

Learn More

Dendy, Christina. *Physical Science*. Abdo, 2025.

Sherman, Suzanne. *The Shocking Story of Electricity*. DK, 2023.

Van Vleet, Carmella. *Electricity*. Nomad, 2022.

Index

About the Author

Megan Gendell is a writer and editor in Minnesota. She loves learning about how things work.